Hungry Like a Cheetah

By Sally Cowan

Ash and Pop were reading a book about animals.

"Pop, pandas are from China," Ash said.

"I know!" said Pop.
"And pandas eat **heaps**
of bamboo!"

"They don't eat beef pie, like us!"
said Ash.

Just then, Ash smelled
a burning smell!

Ash and Pop jumped off the sofa.

"The pie!" shouted Ash.

Pop pulled out the burnt pie.

"I will have to toss it away,"
Pop said.
"Nan will be mad at me!"

"I'm as hungry as a shark!"
said Ash.

"I don't have an extra pie,"
said Pop.
"What can we eat?"

Pop held up a banana
from the fruit bowl.

"I'm not a baboon!" Ash said.

"How about a salad?" said Pop.
"We can eat plants like zebras!"

"I like salad," said Ash.
"But that is not as good
as beef pie!"

Ash looked around.

"I found a tin of mushrooms
and a pack of macaroni!"
she said.

"You can see well, like a cheetah!" said Pop.

"I can smell some feta in here!"
Ash said.

"Elephants smell well, too!"
said Pop.
"Just like you!"

Nan came home in time to eat.

They ate macaroni with mushrooms and feta.

They ate a salad and drank soda.

"This hungry cheetah wants more macaroni!" said Ash.

CHECKING FOR MEANING

1. What were Ash and Pop reading about? *(Literal)*

2. How did Ash know the pie was burning? *(Literal)*

3. How do you know Ash enjoyed eating the macaroni with feta and mushrooms? *(Inferential)*

EXTENDING VOCABULARY

macaroni	What is *macaroni*? Macaroni is a type of pasta. What other types of pasta can you name? E.g. spaghetti, fettuccine, ravioli, penne, lasagna. Explain how these pastas are the same and how they are different.
cheetah	Which group of animals does the *cheetah* belong to? What do you know about cheetahs? How fast can they run? What do they eat? Where do they live?
feta	What is *feta*? Have you eaten feta? What other types of cheese do you like?

MOVING BEYOND THE TEXT

1. How do you feel when you smell something delicious cooking in the oven? Why?

2. Talk to students about the words *carnivore* and *herbivore*. Which animals belong to each group?

3. Discuss why families often have macaroni or other types of pasta in the cupboard.

4. Explain an occasion when you made a meal with your family. What did you make? Was it tasty?

THE SCHWA

| a | e | i | o | u |

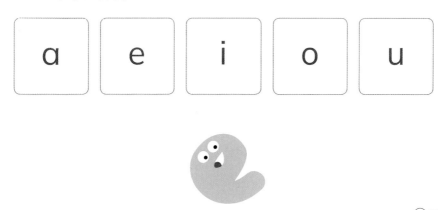

PRACTICE WORDS

a

about

animals

pandas

China

away

sofa

banana

the

baboon

salad

zebras

cheetah

around

macaroni

soda

feta

Elephants

extra

The